Nature-Inspired Innovations

Biomimicry and
MEDICINE

Robin Koontz

Rourke
Educational Media
rourkeeducationalmedia.com

Before & After Reading Activities

Before Reading:

Building Academic Vocabulary and Background Knowledge

Before reading a book, it is important to tap into what your child or students already know about the topic. This will help them develop their vocabulary, increase their reading comprehension, and make connections across the curriculum.

1. *Look at the cover of the book. What will this book be about?*
2. *What do you already know about the topic?*
3. *Let's study the Table of Contents. What will you learn about in the book's chapters?*
4. *What would you like to learn about this topic? Do you think you might learn about it from this book? Why or why not?*
5. *Use a reading journal to write about your knowledge of this topic. Record what you already know about the topic and what you hope to learn about the topic.*
6. *Read the book.*
7. *In your reading journal, record what you learned about the topic and your response to the book.*
8. *After reading the book complete the activities below.*

Content Area Vocabulary

Read the list. What do these words mean?

algorithm
anhydrobiosis
biodegradable
cornea
electrodes
exoskeleton
parasitic
polymer
proboscis
prosthetic
rehydrated
synthetic
virtual

After Reading:

Comprehension and Extension Activity

After reading the book, work on the following questions with your child or students in order to check their level of reading comprehension and content mastery.

1. *What has nature done that inspired biomimics in the medical field? (Summarize)*
2. *What other applications outside of medicine could work using the bombardier beetle spray mechanism? (Infer)*
3. *What does seaweed do that would inspire a polymer material that rehydrates like a sponge? (Asking Questions)*
4. *How would stitches that are biodegradable help you? (Text to Self Connection)*
5. *Why does a new medical product have to be tested before anyone can get it? (Infer)*

Extension Activity

Think of a new or improved medical product or procedure that mimics the action of a frog's tongue. How would it work? Does it improve on something or create something new?

Table of Contents

Medical Marvels

If a bombardier beetle feels threatened, it blasts a powerful jet spray of boiling chemicals at its attacker. Its built-in combustion chamber mixes and boils chemicals in its body. The gases from the process create pressure that makes the blast powerful enough to cause serious injury.

This illustration shows a bombardier beetle's protective chamber in its hindquarters where it mixes chemicals.

Researchers are working on ways to mimic the beetle's spray system. They hope to create new kinds of drug delivery systems as well as other spray system applications.

bombardier beetle

Biomimicry, also called biomimetics, involves the study of how functions are delivered in biology, then translating those functions into designs that suit human needs. Architects, scientists, and engineers involved in biomimicry have recognized that nature is the world's largest science and engineering lab.

Nature has 3.8 billion years of experience! Using nature as inspiration and a guide, biomimics research, experiment with, and create innovative designs that help solve human problems.

Biomimicry plays an important role in the medical field with many projects currently being researched and tested. Many of these examples remain in the testing and improving stage before they can be widely available.

Animals, plants, and even microorganisms are the inspiration behind biomimicry. Extensive testing in the lab helps to design and improve on every new medical application.

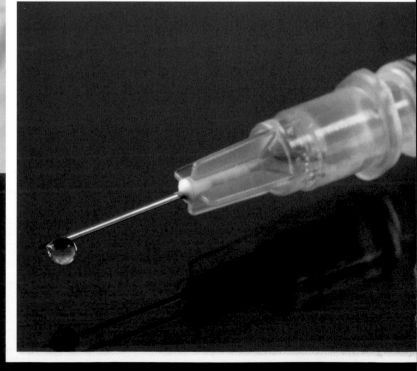

Mosquitoes are considered the deadliest animals in the world. Yet, injectable vaccines are used to prevent many diseases that mosquitoes spread.

A mechanical engineer named Seiji Aoyagi figured out why we can barely feel a mosquito's sharp **proboscis** when it pokes our skin. The outer surface of the proboscis has a jagged, not smooth surface.

The proboscis's jagged surface allows it to stick without touching many nerves in the skin. When he copied the design of the mosquito's proboscis, Seiji created an almost pain-free hypodermic needle.

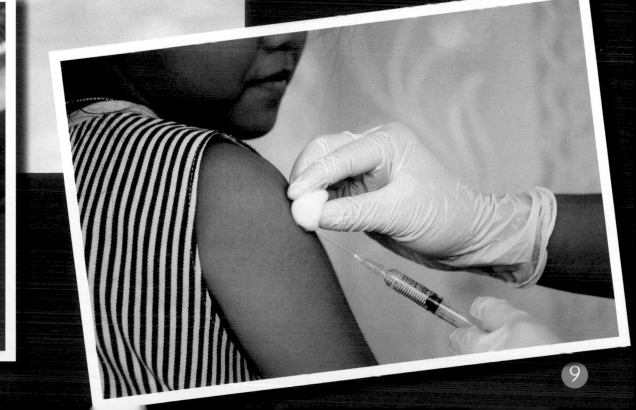

Tardigrades, also called water bears, are microscopic animals that can survive severe cold, high pressure, and high levels of radiation. Tardigrades can even survive without food or water for more than a hundred years. Their bodies use a process called **anhydrobiosis** that protects them until they are **rehydrated**.

Water bears are also called moss piglets, as some live in droplets of water on moss and lichens. They are found everywhere in the world from high in the mountains to deep in the sea.

A company called Biomatrica has already mimicked anhydrobiosis to protect live vaccines when refrigeration is not available. The chemical barrier wraps the vaccine and protects it until it is ready to be used. This water-bear-inspired process makes it easier to transport and store vaccines in tropical countries where dependable refrigeration is not available.

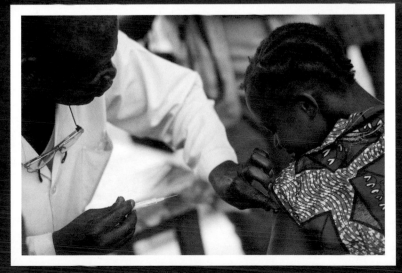

Vaccines being given in the Congo are helping to curtail the spread of several diseases.

Some of the most unlikely animals have become inspiration for biomimics. Thanks to modern methods of discovery and exploration, scientists can get closer to animals than they ever could before.

A sea cucumber is a tubular-looking spiny creature related to starfish. Working as a cleaning service, it crawls around on the sea floor and eats whatever it runs across. Sea cucumbers have soft bodies that can easily change shape and size. They can also quickly change from soft-bodied to stiff, like hard plastic, to keep from being eaten. That ability is what caught the attention of biomimic researchers.

There are about 1,250 species of sea cucumbers, some spinier than others. They live in both shallow and deep ocean waters.

sea cucumber

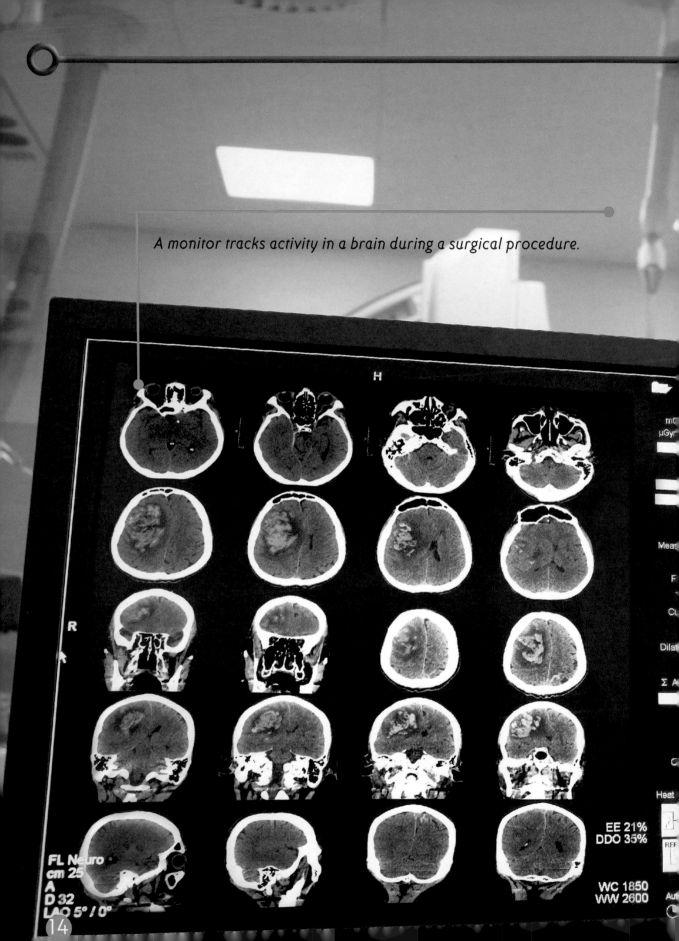

A monitor tracks activity in a brain during a surgical procedure.

The unique skin structure of a sea cucumber allows it to perform its amazing trick. Scientists mimicked that structure for a new kind of plastic **polymer**. The material is rigid when dry and becomes flexible when it's wet. They hope to use the sea cucumber-inspired material to create flexible **electrodes** used to treat brain injuries.

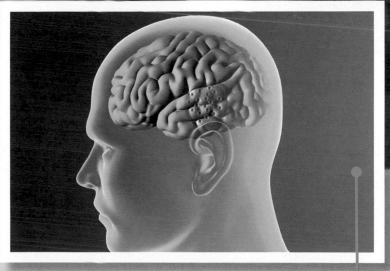

Traditional electrodes are metal or plastic and can cause tissue damage. A flexible electrode would be less damaging to sensitive brain tissue.

Pacific sea nettle jellyfish

Jeffrey Karp is a bioengineer who, along with his team members, has designed a lot of bio-inspired inventions. Jellyfish tentacles inspired one system. Blood flowed too fast through special devices that were employed to detect cancer cells. So, Jeffrey created tiny jellyfish-like tentacle devices that could grab targeted, possibly cancerous cells.

> " We don't sit in front of the jellyfish tank and think, 'How can we design a medical device that does what these jellyfish do?' It's more like, we have a problem we need to solve, and these floating piles of jelly might be able to help us. " —Jeffrey Karp

Scientist David J. Mooney designed a polymer sponge that is injected into the body. Once inside, the sponge rehydrates much like a real sponge. It fills space where tissue has been removed and promotes healing. His idea, still under testing, was inspired by seaweed's behavior.

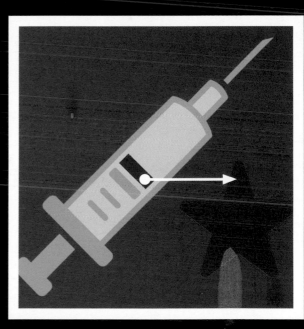

Harvard bioengineers cut out stars, squares, and hearts and pushed them through a syringe to demonstrate their gel-based sponge. This sponge, once injected into a body, regains its original shape and slowly releases drugs or stem cells before safely degrading.

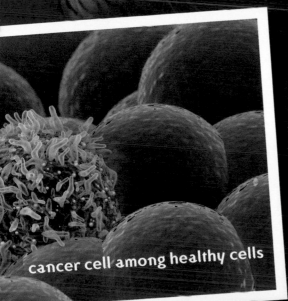

cancer cell among healthy cells

Nature-Made
Bandages and Stitches

Glues inspired by gecko feet are an early form of biomimicry. But Jeffrey Karp figured out a way to use the same concept to create gecko-inspired bandages.

Biodegradable gecko bandages have a textured surface that mimics the bumpy bottoms of gecko feet. The designers came up with a bio-rubber material that made the gecko bandage safer to use on live tissue.

Maria Pereira was one of Jeffrey Karp's graduate students. He asked her to help design a special glue that could be used to stitch heart defects in young patients. The glue would need to quickly form a perfect seal as well as withstand a beating heart with blood flowing around it. The glue also had to be nontoxic and biodegradable, since it would be inside the body.

The researchers studied how slugs and snails excrete slime that allows them to travel on wet surfaces without falling. Maria and Jeffrey focused on a marine sandcastle worm that also secretes a water-repelling sticky goo.

"Nature is the best problem-solver." —Jeffrey Karp

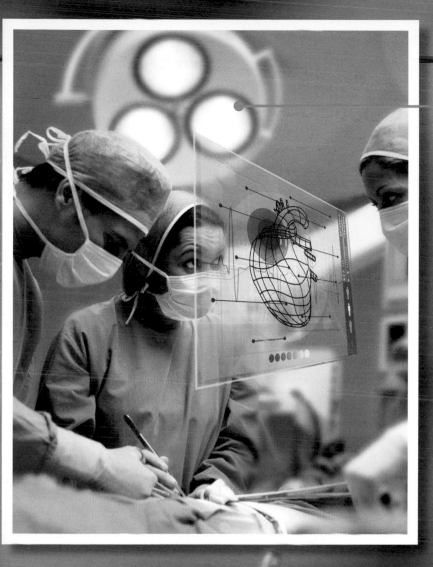

Stitching a heart during surgery is risky and difficult. The bio-inspired glue bonds quickly and lets the heart heal on its own without stitches.

After years of experimenting, they developed a liquid surgical glue that is being tested for many medical applications. The amazing bio-inspired surgical glue was recently approved for use in Europe.

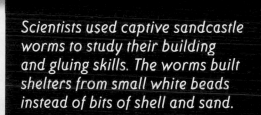

Scientists used captive sandcastle worms to study their building and gluing skills. The worms built shelters from small white beads instead of bits of shell and sand.

Sandcastle worms create underwater shelters with sand and other minerals that they glue together with their secretions. Their structures have inspired biomimicry scientists with new ways to glue together shattered bone fragments.

Spiders spin a fiber silk that is stronger than any other nature-made or man-made fiber. Spider silk is also stretchable and lightweight. They use the silk to make webs or nets to catch prey.

Spiders produce the protein-based silk through ducts in their bodies. The energy-absorbing threads they produce can be radically stretched and altered without breaking. It's no wonder biomimics have studied spider silk for ideas and inspiration!

Glands inside the spider produce several kinds of liquid silk. The silk is released from tiny nozzles called spinnerets on the back side of the spider's abdomen.

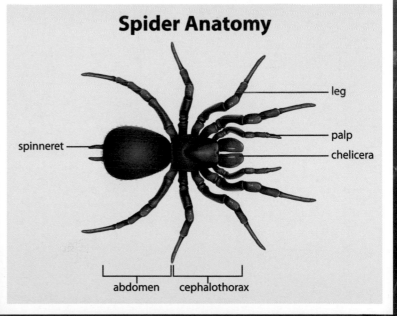

Spider Anatomy

spinneret

leg

palp

chelicera

abdomen   cephalothorax

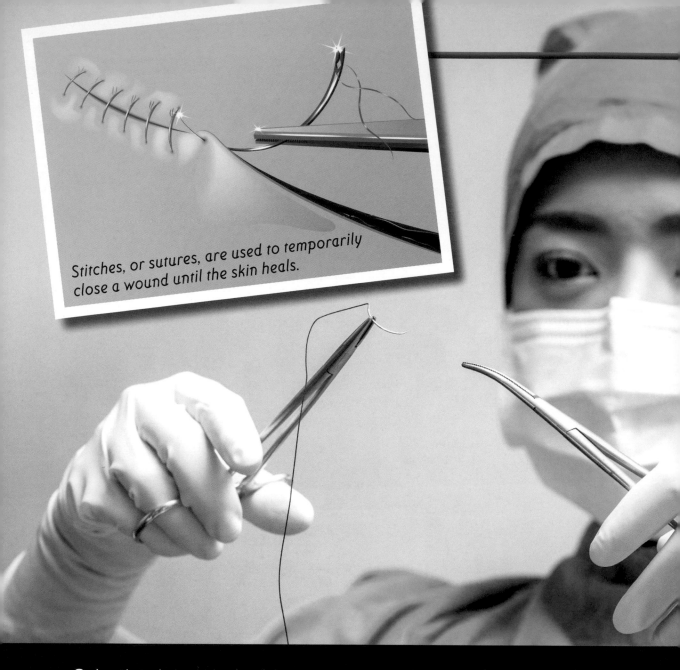

Stitches, or sutures, are used to temporarily close a wound until the skin heals.

Scientists have worked for years to develop **synthetic** silk similar to spider silk. Synthetic spider silk could be used to stitch wounds and tendons. It would be biodegradable as well as inexpensive to manufacture.

Jeffrey Karp and his team also came up with surgical staples that were inspired by a **parasitic** worm. The worm sticks its proboscis

into a fish and inflates the tip so the worm can hang on for the ride. The bio-inspired staples work in much the same way. Tiny needles react with water, causing the needle tips to swell and lock into place.

Porcupine quills also inspired Jeffrey. He and his team created a new kind of medical needle. Barbed like a porcupine quill, the design doesn't puncture surrounding tissue because it doesn't need much force to penetrate the intended area.

porcupine

Animal-Inspired Limbs

horsehead
grasshopper

Scientists studying horsehead grasshoppers and locusts found that passive joint forces vary between the middle and hind legs. The passive joint forces allow energy to transfer from the stronger to the weaker muscles.

Some insects power their movements using more than just muscles. Engineers are studying insects to find out how they control their actions. They discovered that many insects use forces from their joints that work without using muscles.

The scientists hope that by continuing to study how insect limbs are controlled, they can create **prosthetic** limbs that function in similar ways.

locust

Designer Kaylene Kau looked to nature to find new ideas for prosthetic limbs and found inspiration in the deep sea: the octopus! An octopus tentacle grasps an object by wrapping around it.

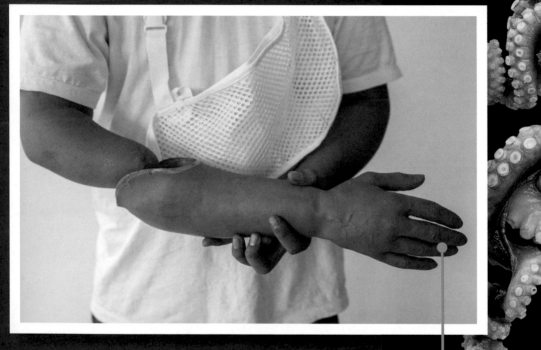

A tentacle-inspired arm will attach much like traditional prosthetics.

Kaylene's tentacle-inspired prosthetic arm is designed to fit over an existing arm as a way to complement the human arm's limited function. It is run by a motor and cables and controlled by the user.

Kaylene's design would curl and grab hold of objects similar to the way an octopus tentacle operates.

Kiisa Nishikawa, a biologist, was inspired by the way a frog snatches a bug with its tongue. Frogs can make that split-second movement because of a spring-like muscle. The muscle can stretch and shorten so fast the frog's brain isn't even involved in the action.

To mimic how a frog tongue works, a group of scientists at Northern Arizona University designed a special **algorithm** for a computer chip. The algorithm they wrote causes a computer chip to act like a **virtual** muscle that controls the movement of a prosthetic or a robotic limb. The artificial device would imitate the way real muscles work.

Ana Carolina Alves is working to create artificial arms and hands that can be manufactured using a 3D printer. Her team studied functions in nature to get ideas for their new design. Two animals, the chiton and the armadillo, were the most inspiring for their project.

66 When we look at nature, we are not trying to replace a hand, but to replace the function of a hand. 99

Ana Carolina Alves

An armadillo has tough overlapping plates that work together for flexible movement. The marine chiton has an **exoskeleton** with overlapping shells, like an armadillo. Their movements are not like the ball-and-socket joints in a traditional prosthesis. A design based on these animals could give the user more function. Ana and her team are working with others to plan and test their new design.

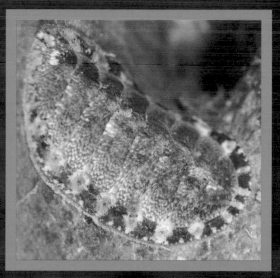
marine chiton

armadillo

Pit vipers inspired a new kind of artificial skin for prosthetic limbs. Pit vipers have two heat-sensing pit organs located between the eye and nostril. The poisonous snake can sense the heat from prey without using its sight. The new material being tested can detect temperature changes in a similar way.

The snake-inspired material could also be used in first-aid bandages so health professionals would be alerted to an increase in temperature, which is a sign of infection.

heat-sensing organ

Bio-Cleaning Ideas

tiger shark

Sharks have inspired several biomimicry projects. A shark's skin has millions of tiny, overlapping, tooth-like scales called dermal denticles. The tiny grooves on the scales align with the water flow as the shark swims. The shark can swim fast without using much energy.

Researchers mimicked shark skin by creating a paint that saves fuel costs for airplanes, ships, and automobiles.

Those same denticles have another function. Because of the reduced drag when the shark swims, microorganisms that can harm the shark can't hitch a ride very easily.

Sharklet Technologies borrowed from shark skin to create surface materials that repel germs. Since those bad bugs can't grow, the material is perfect for use in environments that need to be sterile, such as hospitals, public bathrooms, and restaurant kitchens.

The term dermal denticle *translates to "skin teeth," and this magnified view of shark denticles shows they do look like teeth!*

Cicada wings appear smooth, but they are not. A cicada's wing surface has billions of microscopic spikes called *nanospikes*. Microscopic bacteria spear themselves to death if they land on one of these spiky wings. This discovery of a natural material that destroys bacteria was an inspiration to researchers.

A covering that mimicked a cidada wing's structure could be used to kill any bacteria or virus that land on it. The germ-killing material could possibly eliminate the need for cleaning chemicals.

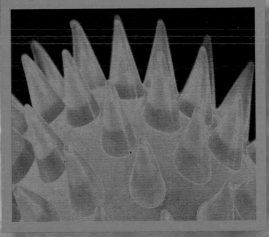

A surface material with microscopic spikes could kill viruses and bacteria by puncturing their membranes, keeping the surface sterile without chemicals.

cornea

Bioengineers also mimicked a cicada wing to create a plastic **cornea** transplant. The cornea would have the ability to kill germs that landed on it. The nanospike-shaped plastic could also be designed for use in other medical devices.

Biomimicry is inspiring nearly every aspect of the diverse medical field. Scientists still have a lot to learn from the natural world for new, improved, more efficient, and safer ways to address all of our medical needs.

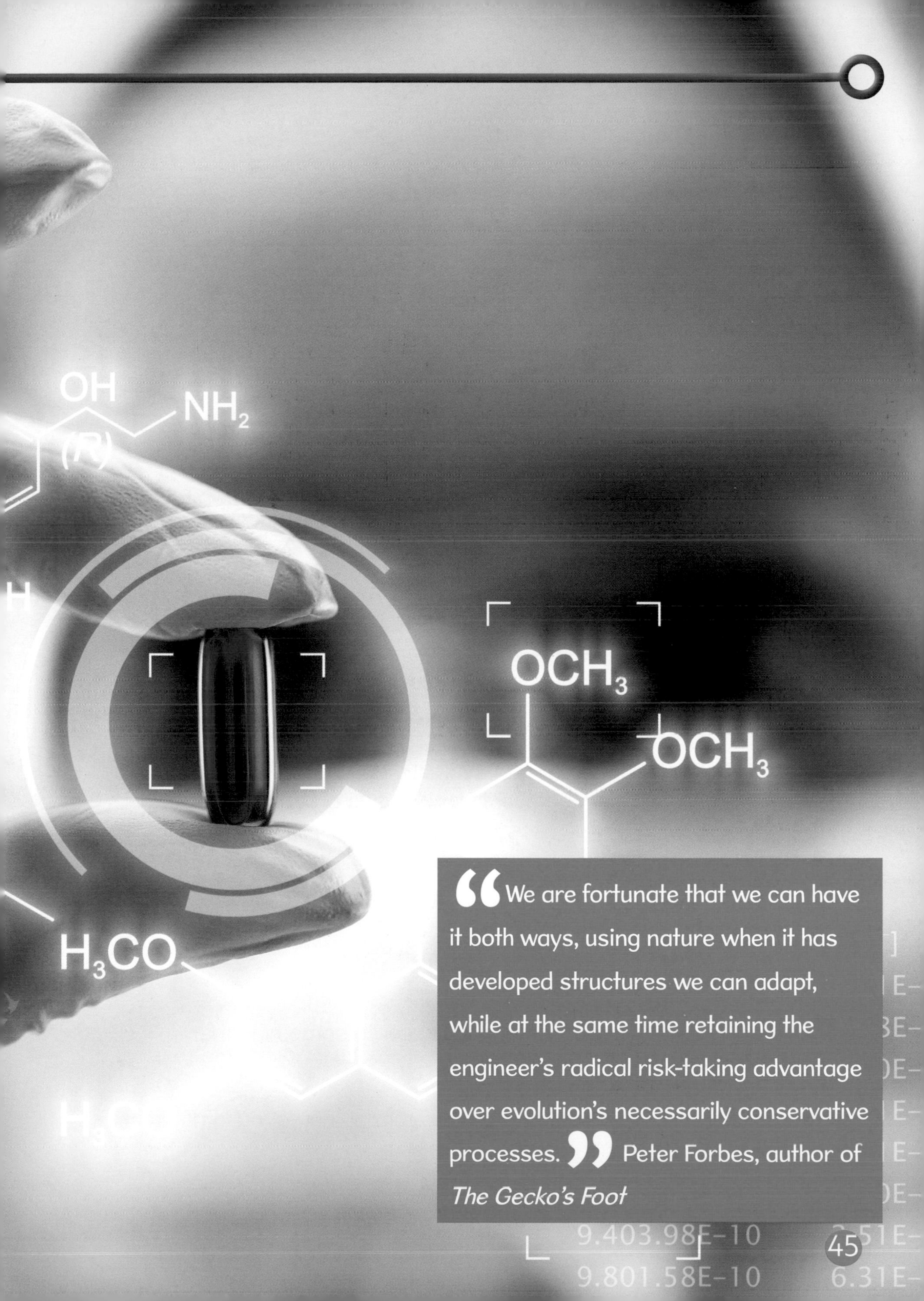

OH

NH₂

(R)

OCH₃

OCH₃

H₃CO

H₃CO

9.403.98E-10

9.801.58E-10   6.31E

Glossary

algorithm (alg-uh-riTH-uhm): a process or set of rules to be followed in calculations or other problem-solving operations, especially by a computer

anhydrobiosis (an-hye-druh-bye-OH-siss): a dormant state induced by drought

biodegradable (bye-oh-di-GRAY-duh-buhl): something that can be broken down naturally by bacteria

cornea (KOR-nee-uh): the transparent outer layer of the eyeball, covering the iris and pupil

electrodes (i-LEK-trodes): points through which electric current can flow in or out of a device or substance

exoskeleton (ek-soh-SKEL-uh-tuhn): a rigid external body covering that provides support and protection

parasitic (pa-ruh-sit-ik): when something gets its food by living on or inside another animal or plant

polymer (POL-uh-mur): a natural or synthetic compound made up of small, simple molecules linked together in long chains of repeating units

proboscis (pruh-BISS-kuhss): a long, sucking mouthpart that is usually tubular and flexible

prosthetic (pross-THET-ik): when an artificial device replaces a missing part of the body

rehydrated (ri-HYE-drayt-uhd): supplied water to something that was dehydrated

synthetic (sin-THET-ik): something that is artificial, not found in nature

virtual (VUR-choo-uhl): almost as described

Index

Show What You Know

1. Why doesn't it hurt when a mosquito bites?
2. Why were medical bioengineers inspired to mimic a sea cucumber?
3. What two things did scientists design that was based on cicada wings?
4. What is the strongest known natural material on Earth?
5. What part of a parasitic worm inspired scientists to invent a new kind of staple?

Further Reading

Benyus, Janine, *Biomimicry: Innovation Inspired by Nature*, Harper Perennial, 2002.

Lee, Dora, *Biomimicry: Inventions Inspired by Nature*, Kids Can Press, 2011.

Yomtov, Nel, *From African Plant to Vaccine Preservation*, Cherry Lake Publishing, 2014.

About the Author

Robin Koontz is a freelance author/illustrator of a wide variety of nonfiction and fiction books, educational blogs, and magazine articles for children and young adults. Her 2011 science title, *Leaps and Creeps - How Animals Move to Survive*, was an Animal Behavior Society Outstanding Children's Book Award Finalist. Raised in Maryland and Alabama, Robin now lives with her husband in the Coast Range of western Oregon where she especially enjoys observing the wildlife on her property. You can learn more on her blog: robinkoontz. wordpress.com.

Meet The Author!
www.meetREMauthors.com

www.rourkeeducationalmedia.com

PHOTO CREDITS: Cover top 3 photos left to right: Sebastian Kaulitzk, Bachkova Natalia, A3pfamily, test tubes © Romolo Tavani; page 4-5 © johannviloria, inset photo © By KASIRA SUDA, illustration inside inset © Blue Door Education; page 6-7 closeup © Syda Productions, full spread © JoeZ; page 8-9 mosquito © Bachkova Natalia, vaccination © A3pfamily, needle © RG-vc; page 10-11 tardigrade © Dotted Yeti; vaccine © Valeriya Anufriyeva; Page 12-13 scuba diver © e2dan, sea cucumber © Rich Carey; page 14-15 brain surgery © sfam_photo, brain illustration © Naeblys; page 16-17 jellyfish © H.Tanaka; cancer cell © CI Photos, page 17 illustration © Aha-Soft; page 18-19 © Papa Bravo, gecko foot © Mr.B-king; page 20-23 glue © Timof, snail © Sanit Fuangnakhon, surgery © wavebreakmedia; page 24-25 © Balazs Justin, spider illustration © BlueRingMedia; page 26-27 © Artemida-psy, surgeon © Virojt Changyencham, page 27 porcupine © vanchai; page 28-29 © Dr Morley Read, page 29 © arka38, page 29 scientist © Mila Supinskaya Glashchenko; page 30-31 prosthetic © Light_Sector 7, octopus © wittaya changkaew; page 32-33 © Lightspring, © Cathy Keifer, computer chip © Bluskystudio; page 34-35 © maxuser; page 36 © Vladimir Wrangel, page 37 © IanRedding; page 38-39 © reptiles4all; page 40-41 © le bouil baptiste; page 42-42 main photo © Mary Terriberry, inset close-up © Petr Malyshev; page 44 illustration © Alex Mit, main photo © Scanrail1 All images from Shutterstock.com except: page 23 sandcastle worm © University of Utah https://creativecommons.org/licenses/by-sa/3.0/deed.en; shark skin closeup page 41 © Pascal Deynat/Odontobase https://creativecommons.org/licenses/by-sa/3.0/deed.en

Edited by: Keli Sipperley

Produced by Blue Door Education for Rourke Educational Media. Cover and Interior design by: Nicola Stratford   www.nicolastratford.com

Library of Congress PCN Data

Biomimicry and Medicine / Robin Koontz
(Nature-Inspired Innovations)
 ISBN 978-1-64156-459-5 (hard cover)
 ISBN 978-1-64156-585-1 (soft cover)
 ISBN 978-1-64156-702-2 (e-Book)
Library of Congress Control Number: 2018930486

Rourke Educational Media
Printed in the United States of America, North Mankato, Minnesota